Contents

Introductions	3
Candlestick Patterns	
The Engulfing Bar Pattern	5
The Doji Candlestick Pattern	7
The Dragon Fly Doji Pattern	8
The Gravestone Doji Pattern	9
The Morning Star	10
The Evening Star Candlestick Pattern	11
The Hammer Candlestick Pattern	12
The Shooting Star Candlestick Pattern	13
The Harami Pattern	14
The Tweezers Tops	15
The Tweezers Bottoms	16
Morubozu	17
Piercing Pattern	18
Three White Soldier	19
Three Inside Up	19
Three Outside Up	20
On Neck Pattern	20
Hanging Man	21
Dark Cloud Cover	22
Three Black Crows	23
Three Inside Down	23
Three Outside Down	24
Falling Three Methods	24

Rising Three Methods	**25**
Upside Tasuki Gap	**25**
Downside Tasuki Gap	**26**
Mat Hold Pattern	**26**

01 INTRODUCTION

Candle designs are a necessary piece of s Technical Analysis. Candlestick patterns arise because human activities and responses are designed and continually rehashed.

In this book, you will figure out how to perceive the most significant candlestick patterns, the brain science behind its arrangement, and what do they show when they structure on the market.

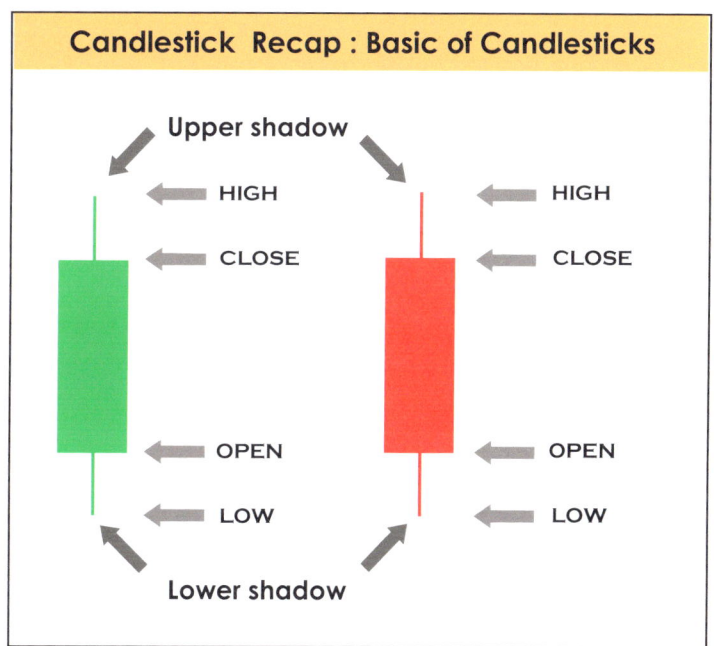

Candlesticks are quite possibly the most remarkable trading concept. They are basic, simple to distinguish, and entirely productive arrangements, research has affirmed that candlesticks have high prescient worth and it delivers positive outcomes.

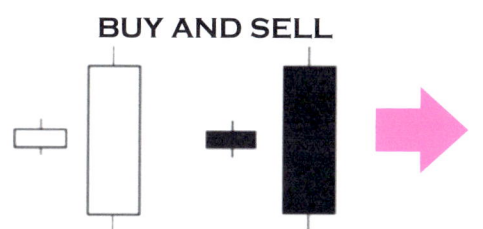

Long bodies allude to solid purchasing or selling pressure, in case there is a candle in which the close candle is above the open with a long body, this demonstrates that purchasers are more grounded and are assuming liability for the market during this timeframe.

3

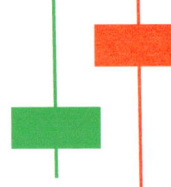

Shadows:

Candlestick with long shadows shows that exchanging activity happened well past the open and close.

The candle has long upper shadow, and short lower shadow, this implies that the increase of buyerd number during that time. Yet, for some explanation, sellers came in and drove the price down to end the meeting back close to its open cost. If the candlestick has a longer lower shadow than the upper shadow, this implies that sellers push the price lower. Yet, for some explanation buyer came in and drove prices back up.

The Engulfing Bar Pattern

The Engulfing bar as it states in its title is framed when it completely overwhelms the previous candlestick. The engulfing bar can engulf more than one candlestick, yet to be viewed as an engulfing bar, at least one candle should be fully consumed. The bearish engulfing pattern is one of the main candlestick patterns.

This candle design comprises two bodies. The principal or first body is smaller than the subsequent ones, as such, the subsequent body engulfs the previous one. See the outline below:

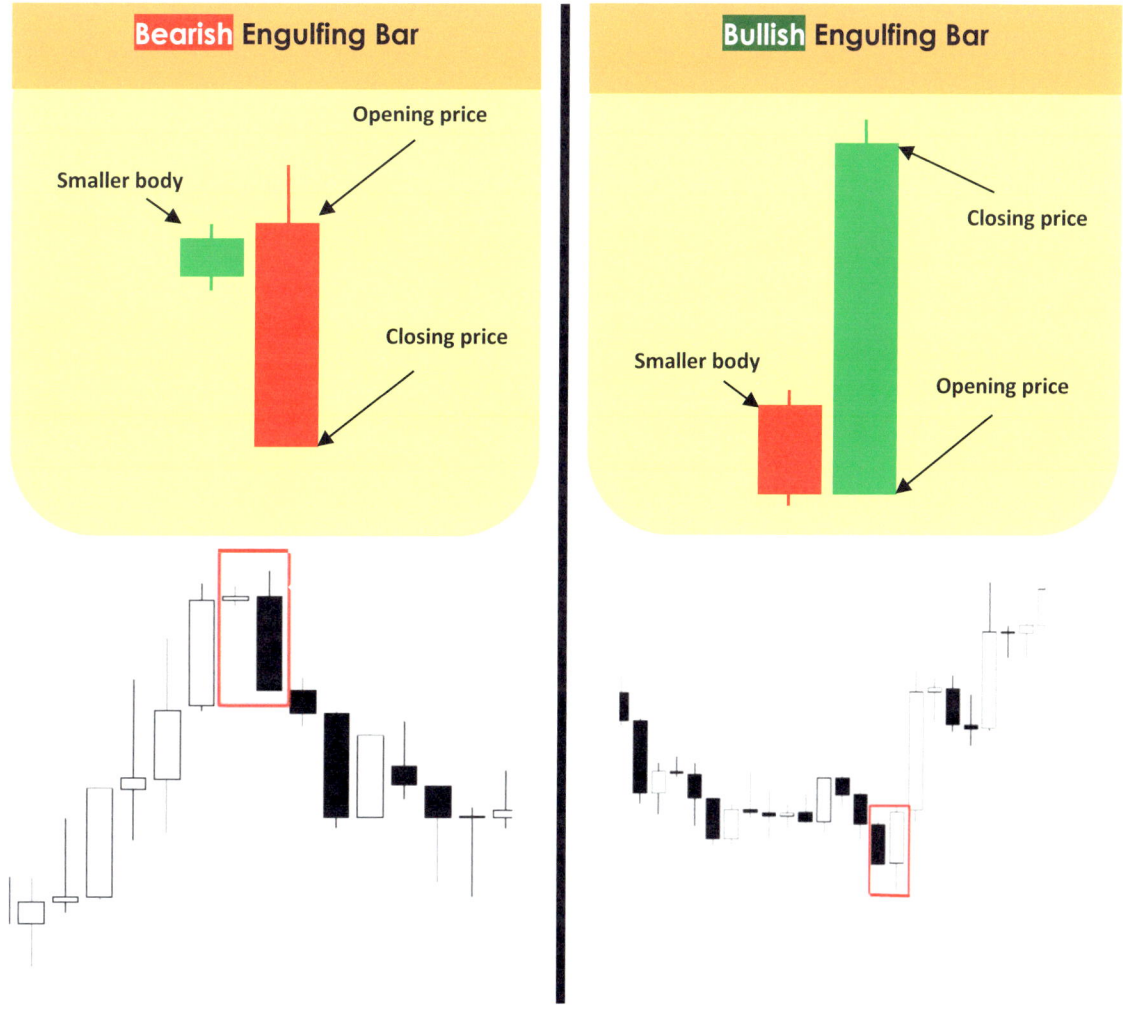

When this price action activity happens in an upswing, we can expect a pattern reversal since buyers are not as yet in charge of the market, and sellers are attempting to push the market to go down. The bullish engulfing bar reveals to us that the market is as of now not taken care of by sellers, and buyers will assume liability for the market. When a bullish engulfing candlestick structures with regards to an upturn, it demonstrates a continuation signal. When bullish engulfing candle structures toward the end of a downtrend, the reversal is much likely to happen.

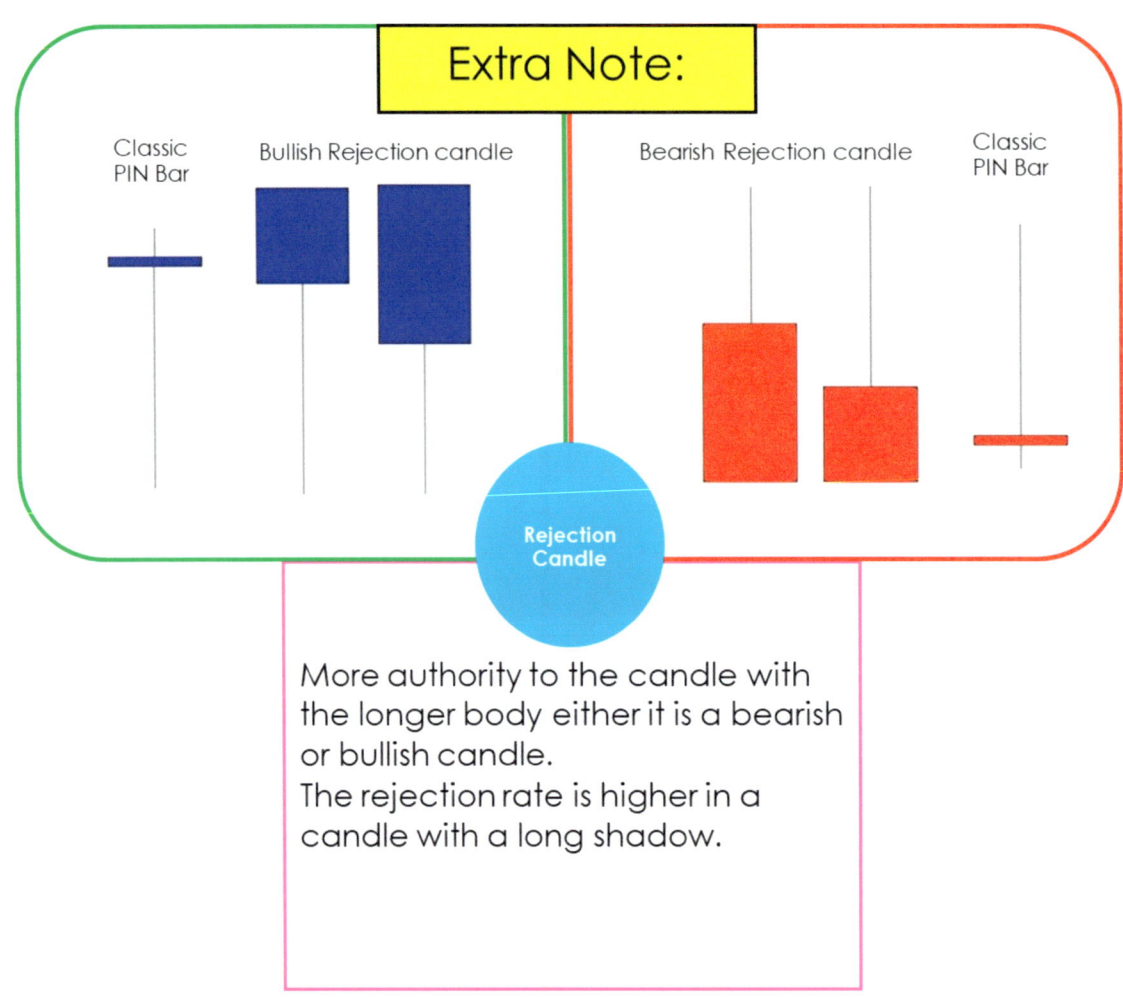

The Doji Candlestick Pattern

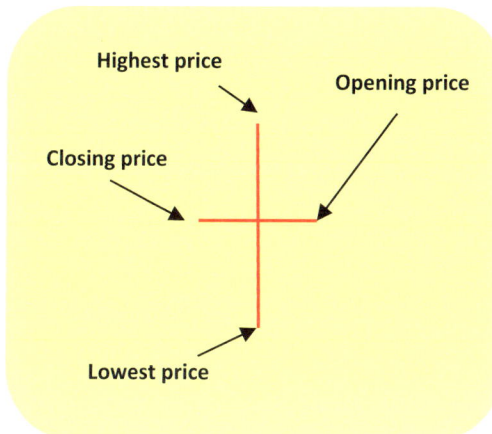

Doji is one of the main Japanese candle patterns, when this candlestick structure, reveals to us that the market opens and closes at a similar price which implies that there is uniformity and uncertainty among buyers and sellerss, no majority trade in the market. The signal indicates that there is no specific movement, where the market will go. It is a reversal pattern.

This diagram shows how the market altered bearing after the appearance of the Doji candlestick. The market was moving up, which implies that buyers were in charge of the market.

The arrangement of the Doji candle shows that buyers can't keep the price higher, and sellers push prices back to the initial value. It is an obvious sign that a reversal pattern is probably going to occur.

Recollect consistently that a Doji shows fairness and hesitation on the market, you will frequently discover it during times of resting after big moves sequential.

At the point when it is found at the base or the highest point of a trend, it is considered as a sign that a current trend is losing its strength.

The Dragon Fly Doji Pattern

The Dragonfly Doji is a **bullish** candle pattern that is framed when the open high and close are something similar or about a similar price. What describes the dragonfly Doji is the long lower tail that shows the opposition of purchasers and their endeavour to push the market up.

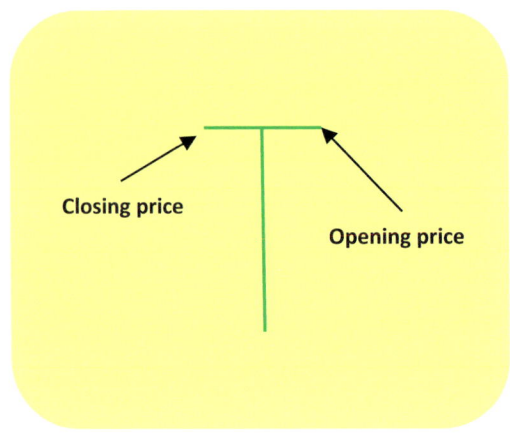

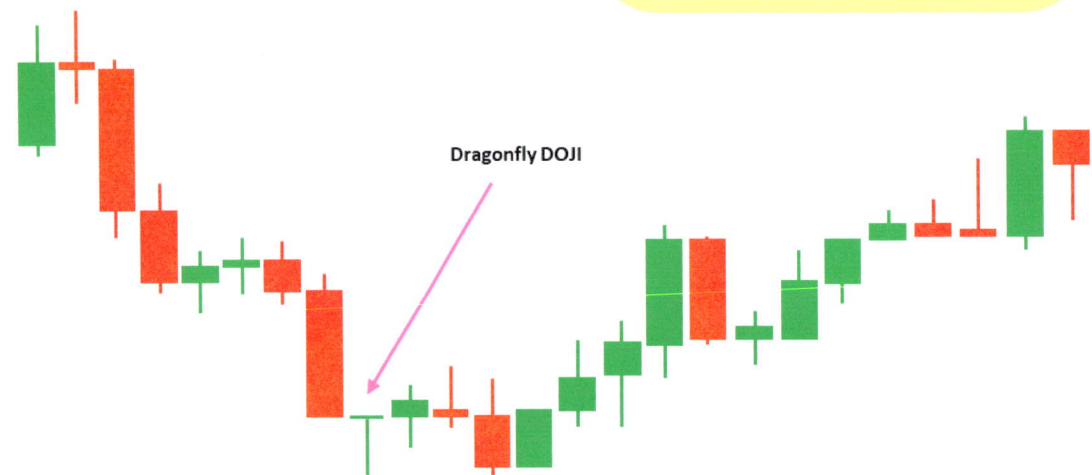

The formation of the Dragonfly Doji with the long lower tail shows us that there is a high purchasing pressure in the area. It always appeared in a downtrend market, whereas changing the trend upward then.

The Gravestone Doji Pattern

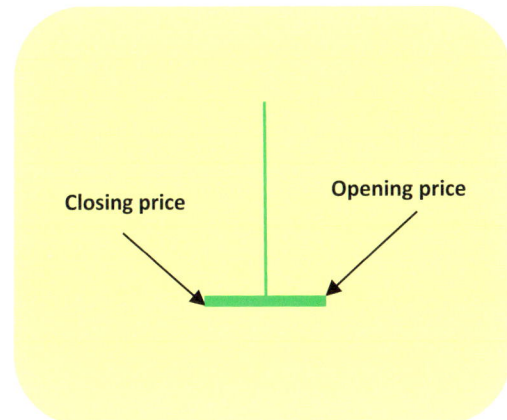

The Gravestone Doji is the **negative** variant of the Dragonfly Doji, it is framed when the open and close are something similar or about a similar price.

What separates the Gravestone Doji from the dragonfly Doji is the long upper tail.

The formation of the long upper tail means that the market is trying an incredible stockpile or obstruction area. (Support and Resistance).

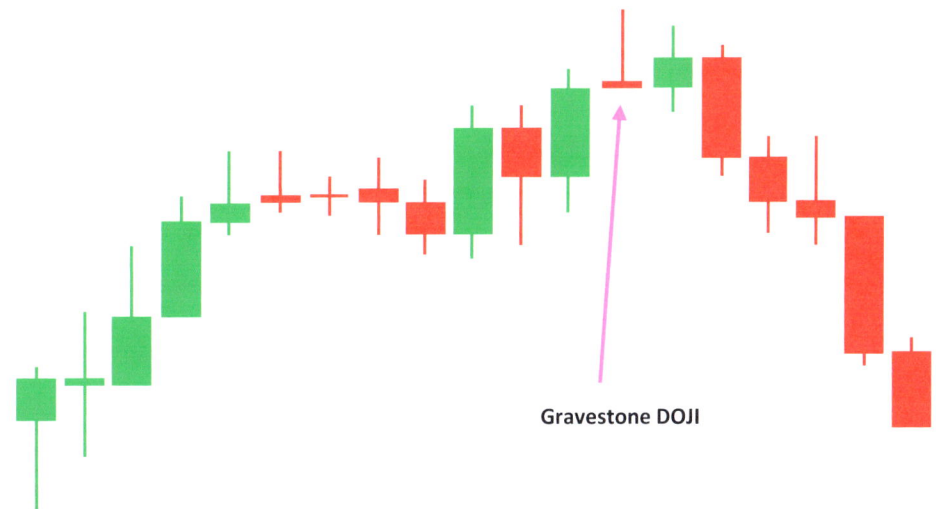

From the chart diagram above, Gravestone Doji found after an uptrend. The formation of this candlestick pattern shows that buyers are not on top of things in the market. For this pattern to be reliable, it should occur near a resistance line.

The Morning Star

This candlestick pattern is known for its Bullish reversal characteristics. Most of the time, it is often spotted at the bottom of the downtrend. A set of morning star patterns consists of three candlesticks.

The 1st candlestick is bearish which indicates that sellers are nonetheless in the rate of the market.

The 2nd candle is a small one that represents that sellers are in control, but they don't push the marketplace an awful lot decrease and this candle may

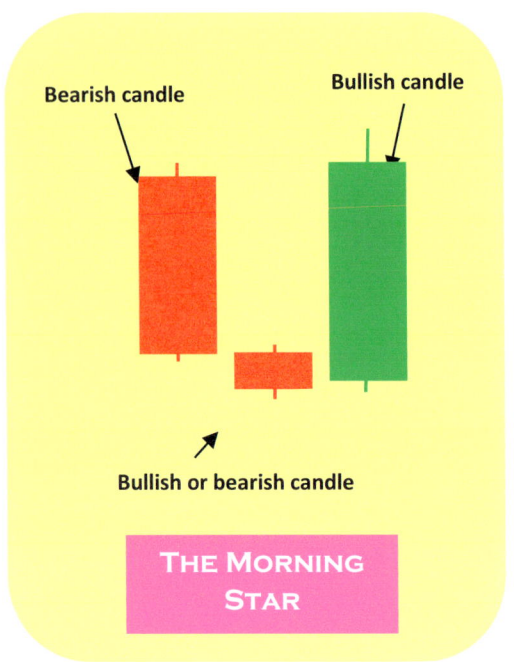

The 3rd candle is bullish that confirm the reversal of the trend. The morning star pattern indicates how buyers took manage of the marketplace from sellers, while this pattern happens at the lowest of downtrend close to the support line, it's far interpreted as an effective trend reversal signal.

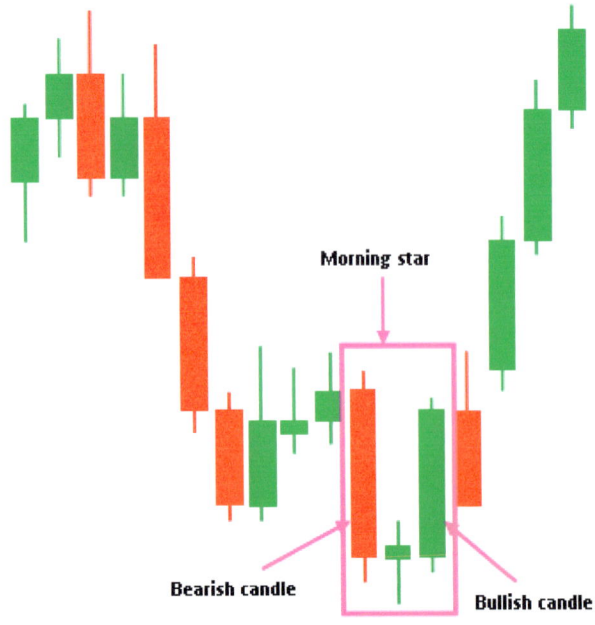

As you can see the pattern befell at an apparent bearish trend. The first candle confirmed the seller's domination, and the second produces indecision within the market, the second candle could be a Doji or any other candle.

But right here, the Doji candle indicated that sellers are suffering to push the market lower. The 3rd bullish candle suggests that buyers are higher than sellers, and the market is likely to reverse.

The Evening Star Candlestick Pattern

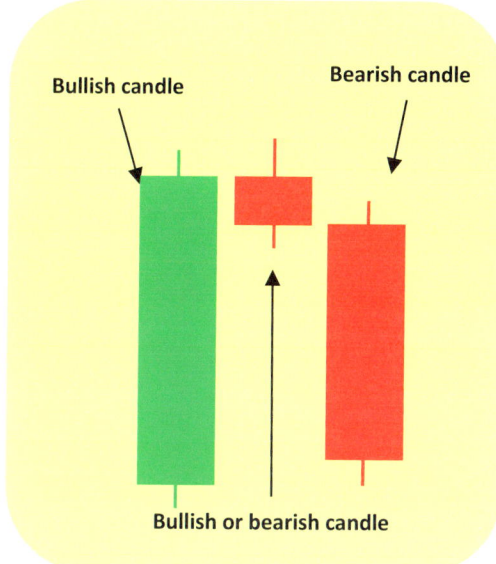

The evening star is a bearish reversal pattern, usually spotted at the top of the trend.

It consist of a set of three candlesticks. The first candle is a green/black candle.

The second candle can be any candle either green, red or Doji candle.

The third candle is a long red (bearish) candle.

The market is moving in uptrend. The first candle shows a significant high price movement. We can see a consolidation of price occurred on the second candle. The trend that created the first long bullish candlestick is starting to fall. The final candlestick gaping decreases than the previous candlestick indicating confirmation of the reversal and the beginning of a brand-new trend down.

The Hammer Candlestick Pattern

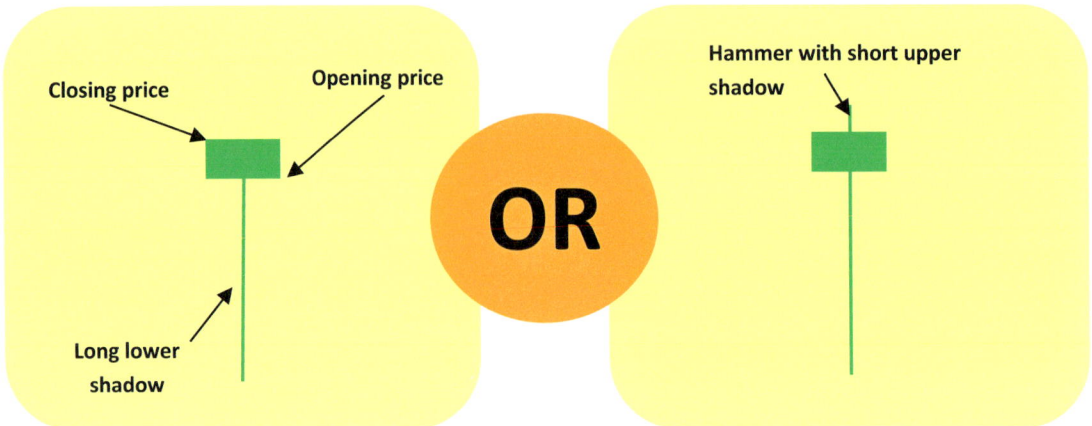

The Hammer candlestick is created whilst the open high and close are kind of the equal price; it is also characterized through a long lower shadow that suggests a bullish rejection from buyers and their goal to push the price up. The hammer candlestick is one of the reversal patterns, usually spotted at the bottom of downtrend.

The hammer patterns are also known as PIN bar.

The Shooting Star Candlestick Pattern

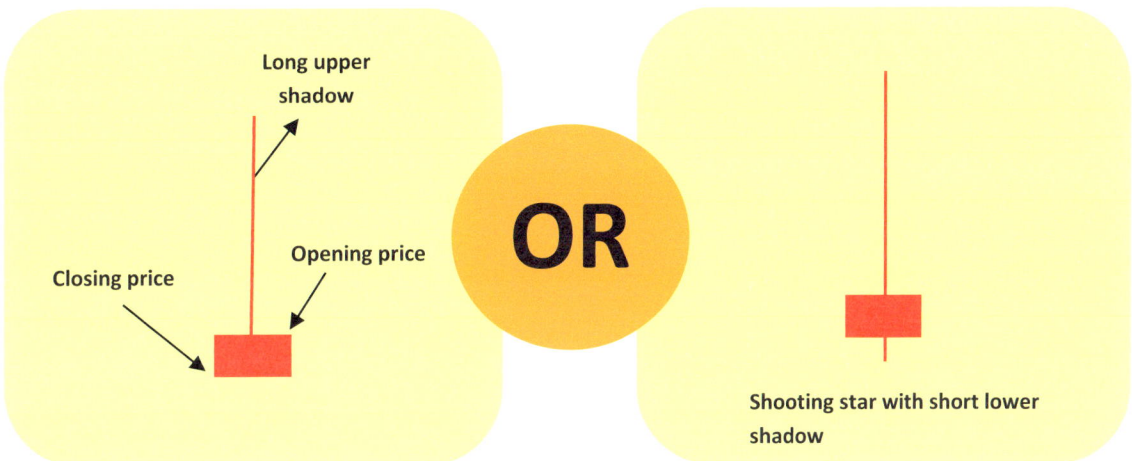

This bearish PIN bar is formed when the open low and close at the same price. Small body, and a long upper shadow. It is the opposite version of the hammer. The shadow ought to be two times the period of the real body or more.

When this pattern is spotted at the uptrend market, the bearish signal is likely to happen most of the time. The shooting star and the morning star is considered as one of the most critical patterns if it forms near resistance line. (High probability set up).

The Harami Pattern

The Harami patterns can be either reversal or continuous signal. The first candle (mother bar) is longer than the second candle (baby bar), covering it totally. These patterns tell us the market is in consolidation.

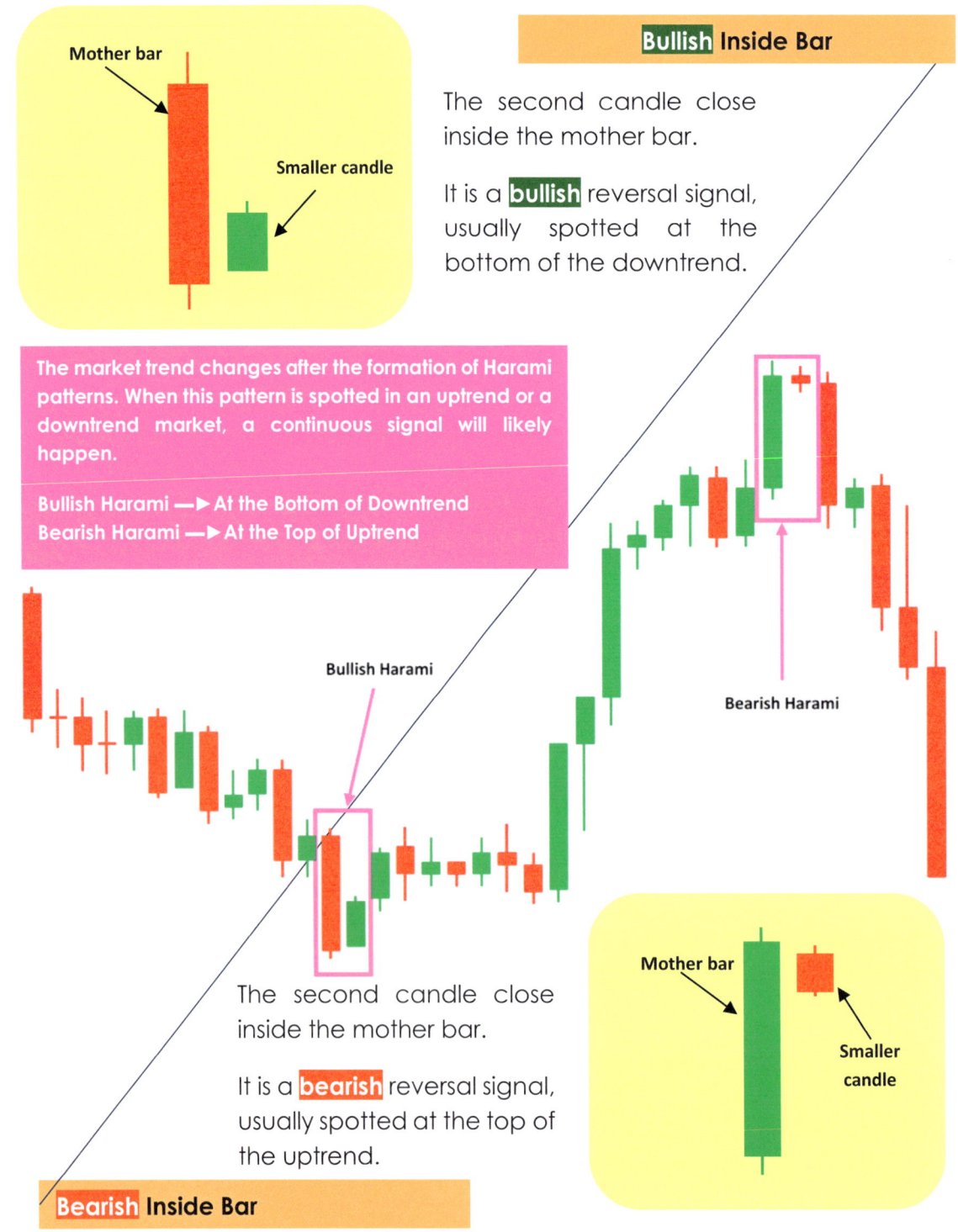

Bullish Inside Bar

The second candle close inside the mother bar.

It is a bullish reversal signal, usually spotted at the bottom of the downtrend.

The market trend changes after the formation of Harami patterns. When this pattern is spotted in an uptrend or a downtrend market, a continuous signal will likely happen.

Bullish Harami ──▶ At the Bottom of Downtrend
Bearish Harami ──▶ At the Top of Uptrend

The second candle close inside the mother bar.

It is a bearish reversal signal, usually spotted at the top of the uptrend.

Bearish Inside Bar

14

The Tweezers Top

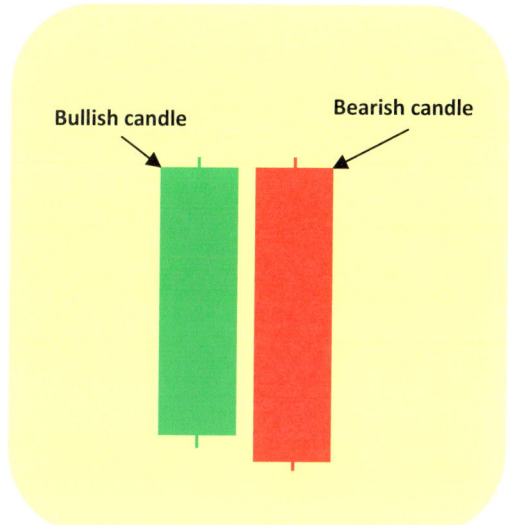

Tweezer Top is a **bearish** reversal pattern. The first candle is green while the second candle is red. It is usually spotted at top of the uptrend, before the price reversing downwards.

Sudden price drop after a high price push by buyers. The second candle is closed lower than the opening price of the first candle.

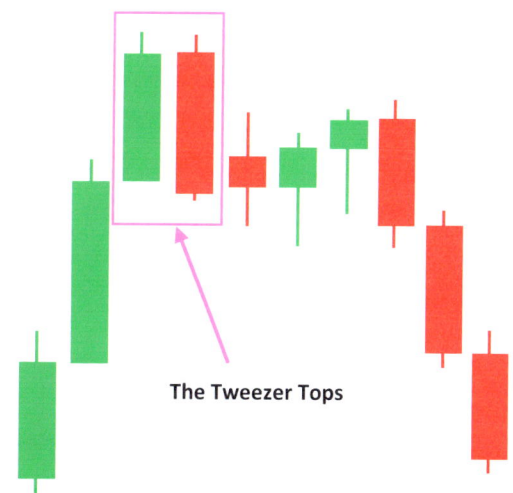

The Tweezer Tops

The Tweezers Bottom

Tweezer Bottom is a **bullish** reversal pattern. The first candle is green while the second candle is red. It is usually spotted at bottom of the downtrend, before the price reversing upwards.

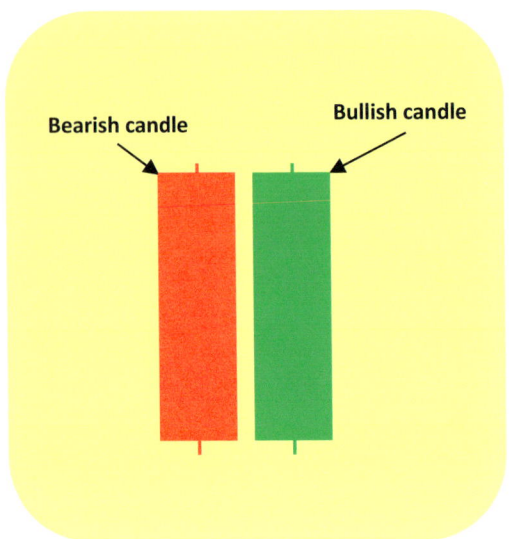

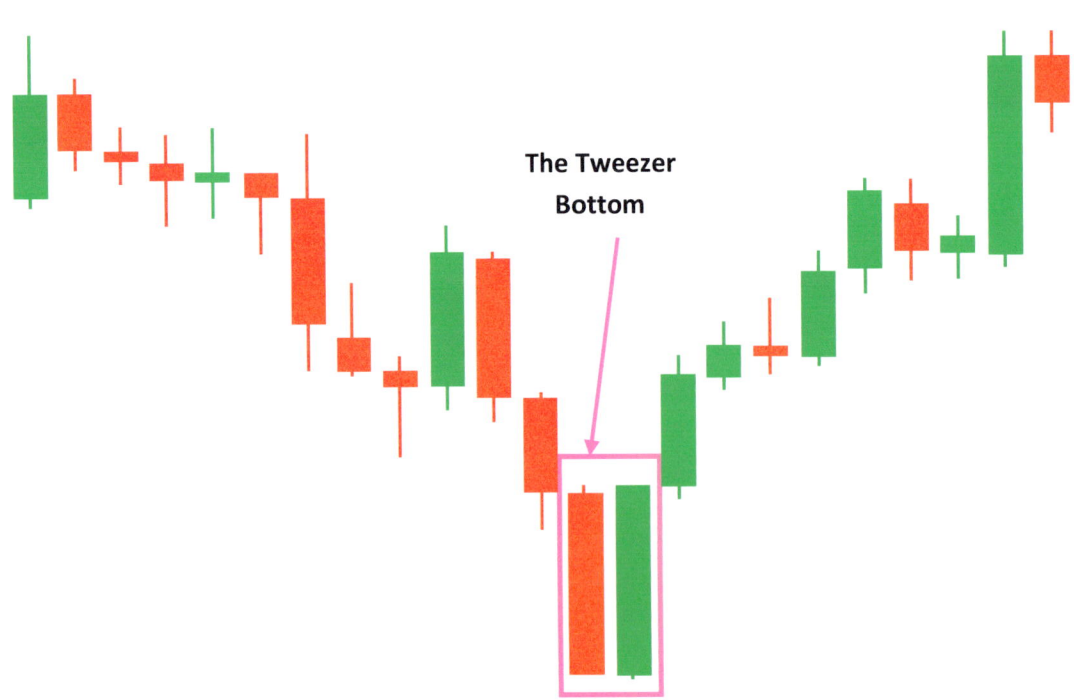

Morubozu

Morubozu is a long candlestick without shadows or at least one of the open or close prices must be flat. Morubozu indicates the market price is moving in one direction. The opening and closing price is equal to the maximum and minimum price respectively.

Bullish Morubozu candlestick indicates high buying interest when the closing price is spotted to be maximum.

Bearish Morubozu candlestick indicates high selling interest when the closing price is spotted to be minimum.

Piercing Pattern

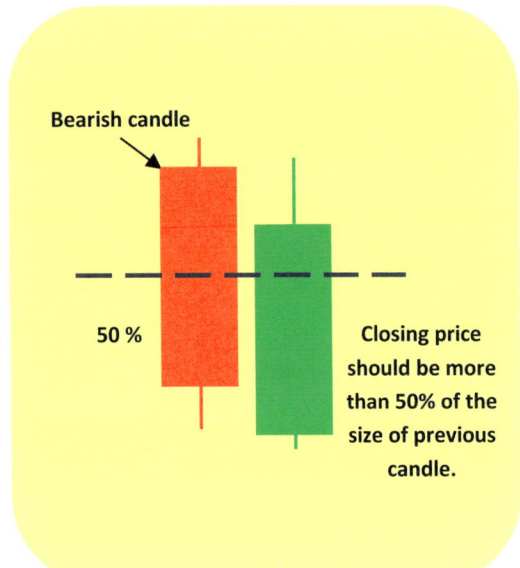

A piercing pattern is a bullish reversal signal, usually spotted after a downtrend.

It consists of two candles. The first candle is bearish, while the second candle is a bullish candle that closes more than half of the real body of the first candle.

The change in trend will take place after price continuation from the first candle.

Three White Soldiers

Three white soldiers is a pattern of three candlesticks or multiple candlesticks that can usually be spotted after a downtrend. It is a **bullish** reversal signal.

The price of each real body is open within the real body of the previous candle.

All of these three candlesticks do not have a long shadow

Three Inside Up

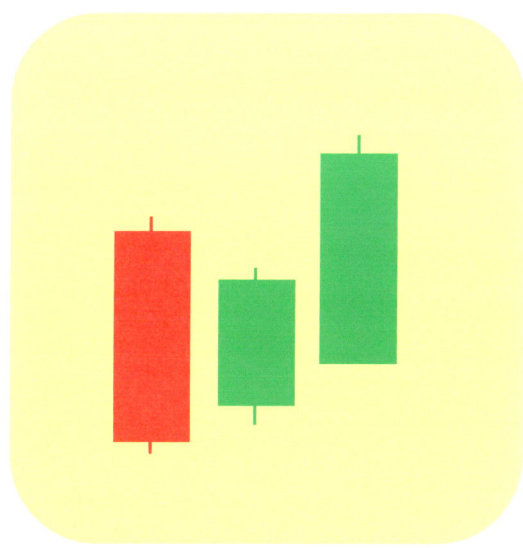

Three Inside up is a **bullish** reversal pattern. It is a set of three candlesticks. The first candle is a long bearish. The second candle should be inside the first candle (within the range of the first candle). The third candle is a long bullish candlestick.

Three Outside Up

Three outside up is a **bullish** reversal signal. It consists of a set of three candlesticks, the first candle is short bearish, the second candle being a long bullish candle covering the first candle. The third candle is a long bullish candle confirming the bullish reversal.

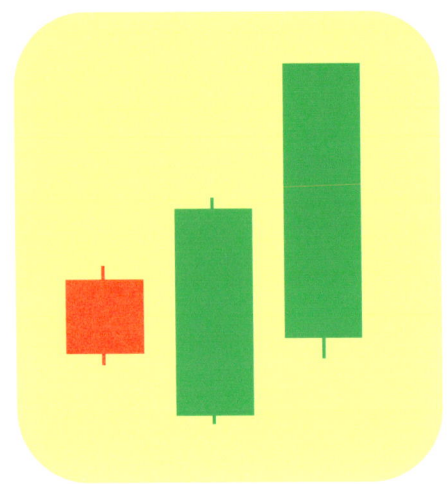

On Neck Pattern

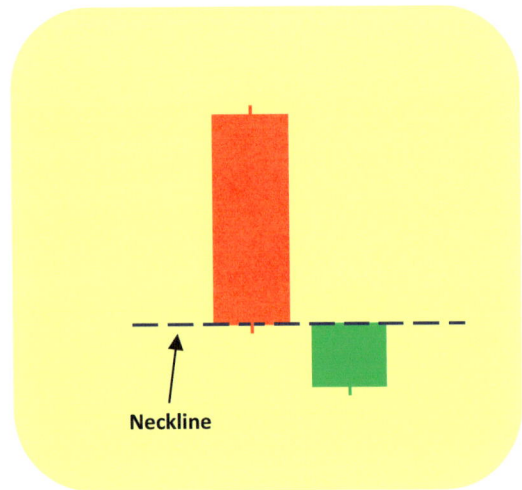

Neckline

The On Neck pattern is usually spotted at the bottom of a downtrend. If we look closely, these two candles close almost the same price across both of these candles forming a horizontal neckline.

There is a price gap on the opening price of the second candle, and then it closes near the closing price of the first candle.

The first bearish candle is a long candle followed by a small bearish candle.

Hanging Man

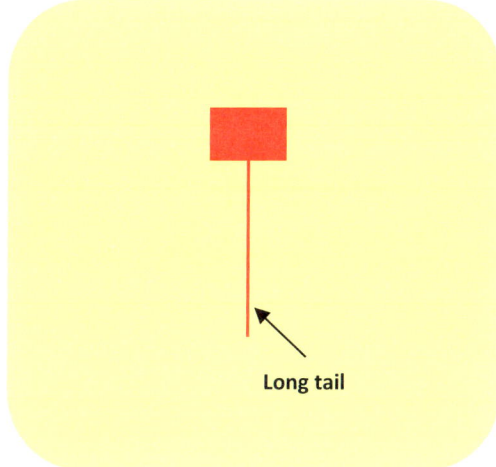

The hanging man is a bearish reversal signal. It is usually spotted at the top of an uptrend. The shadow (tail) of this candlestick must be twice the length of the real body. During this time, selling interest is higher, pushing the price down. Price is going up after that, indicates that buyers suddenly entering the market.

The uptrend is may end as the price will going down.

Dark Cloud Cover

Dark Cloud Cover is the opposite of the piercing pattern. It is a **bearish** reversal signal, usually spotted after an uptrend.

It consists of two candles. The first candle is bullish, while the second candle is a bearish candle that closes more than half of the real body of the first candle.

The change in trend will take place after price continuation from the first candle.

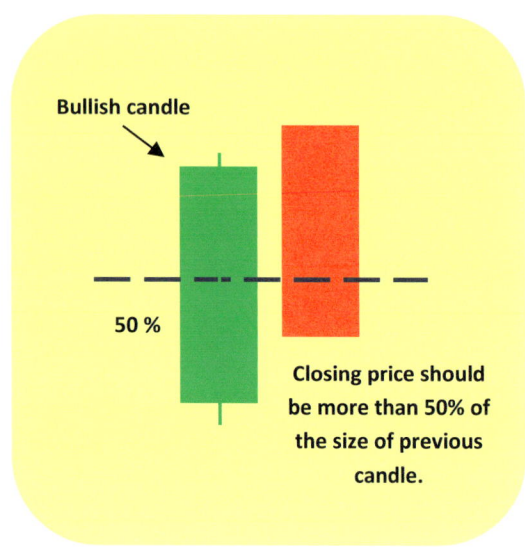

Three Black Crows

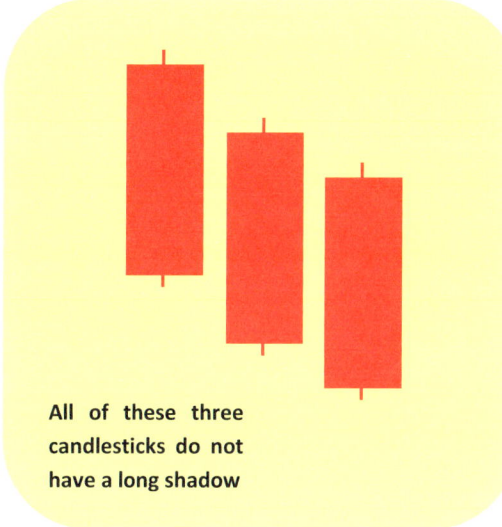

All of these three candlesticks do not have a long shadow

Three black crows is a pattern of three candlesticks or multiple candlesticks that can usually be spotted after an uptrend. It is a **bearish** reversal signal.

The price of each real body is open within the real body of the previous candle.

Three Inside Down

Three Inside up is a **bearish** reversal pattern. It is a set of three candlesticks. The first candle is a long bullish. The second candle should be inside the first candle (within the range of the first candle). The third candle is a long bearish candlestick.

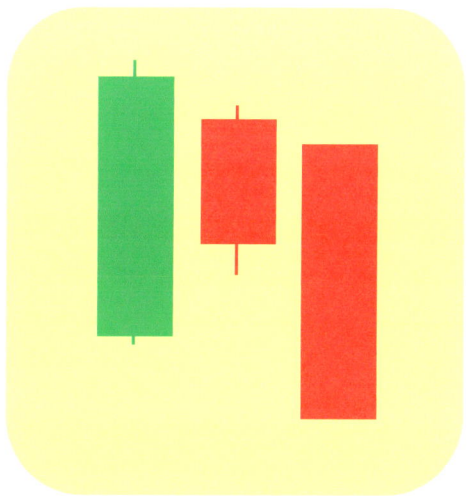

Three Outside Down

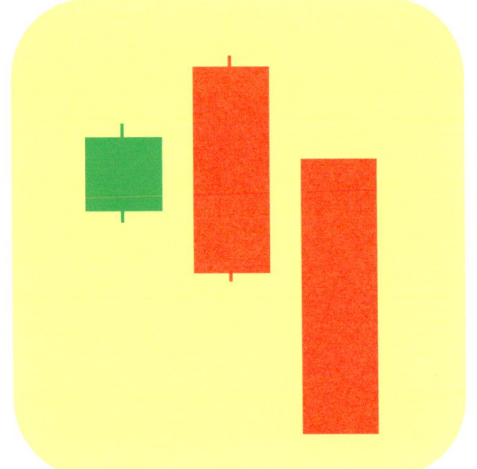

Three outside up is a bearish reversal signal. It consists of a set of three candlesticks, the first candle is short bullish, the second candle being a long bearish candle covering the first candle. The third candle is a long bearish candle confirming the bullish reversal.

Falling Three Methods

The Falling Three Methods is a set of five candles continuous bearish pattern. This pattern indicates an interruption of the prices. However, it is not a reversal pattern, instead the market will continue to bearish.

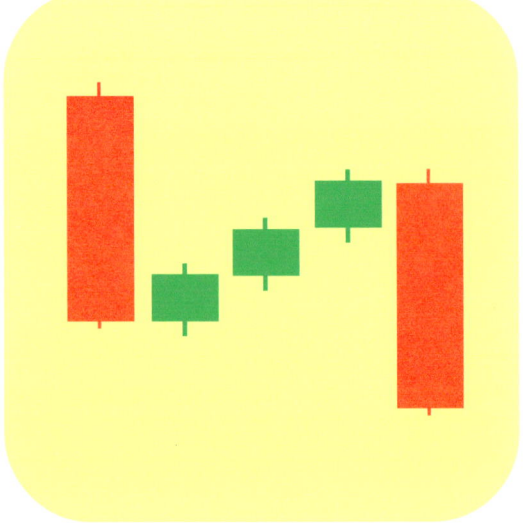

The beginning and end candles are both long bearish candle, with three shorter bullish (counter-trend candle) in the middle.

Rising Three Methods

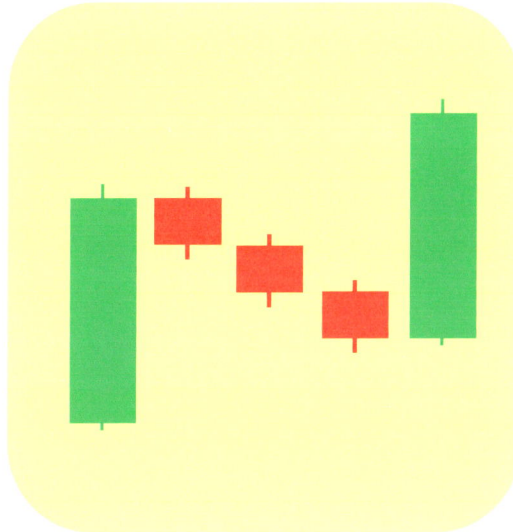

The Rising Three Methods is a set of five candles continuous bullish pattern. This pattern indicates an interruption of the prices. However, it is not a reversal pattern, instead the market will continue to bullish.

The beginning and end candles are both long bullish candle, with three shorter bearish (counter-trend candle) in the middle.

Upside Tasuki Gap

Upside Tasuki Gap is a bullish continuous pattern. It is always spotted in an ongoing uptrend.

The first candle is a long-bodied bullish (without shadow), the second candle also must be bullish and the opening price is gap up to the closing price of the first candle.

The third candle is a bearish that close its price in the gap formed.

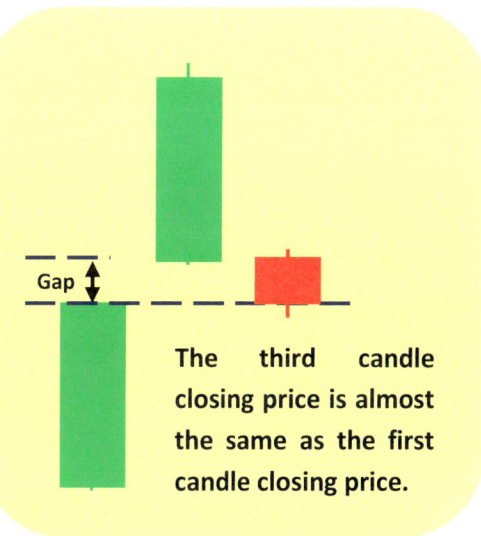

The third candle closing price is almost the same as the first candle closing price.

Downside Tasuki Gap

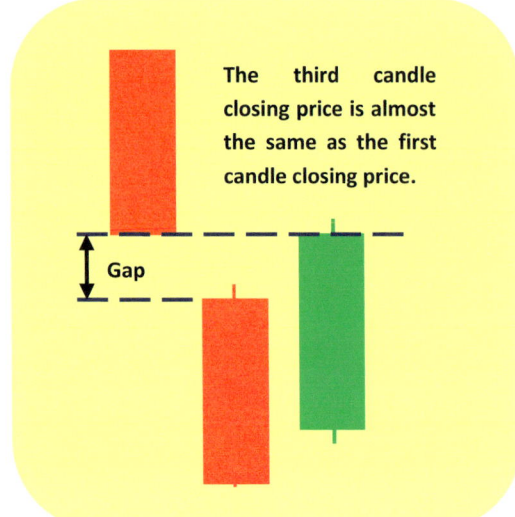

The third candle closing price is almost the same as the first candle closing price.

Gap

Upside Tasuki Gap is a bearish continuous pattern. It is always spotted in an ongoing downtrend.

The first candle is a long-bodied bearish (without shadow), the second candle also must be bearish and the opening price is gap up to the closing price of the first candle.

The third candle is a bullish that close its price in the gap formed.

Mat Hold Pattern

A Mat-Hold pattern is set of multiple candlesticks indicating a continuation of a current trend.

There must be a gap between the closing price of the first candle and the second candle. Three smaller candles move above the low of the first candle.

The last candle is a long bullish (moving upwards).

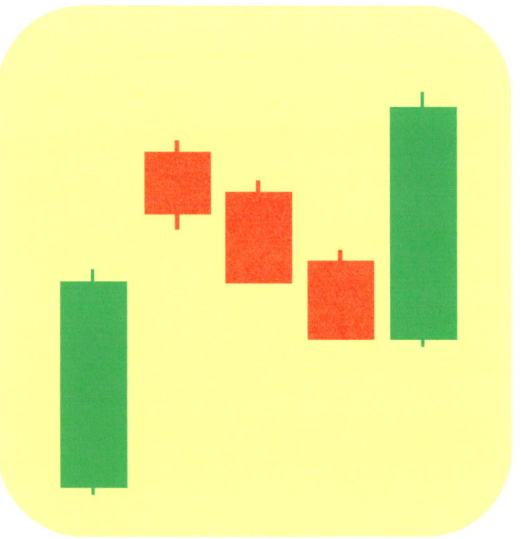

Made in the USA
Columbia, SC
05 November 2024

45751340R00015